LAYERS OF LEARNING

YEAR ONE • UNIT ELEVEN

EARLY JAPAN
MOUNTAINS
STATES OF MATTER
LINE & SHAPE

HooDoo Publishing
United States of America
©2014 Layers of Learning
Copies of maps or activities may be made for a particular family or classroom.
ISBN 978-1494909710

Units At A Glance: Topics For All Four Years of the Layers of Learning Program

1	History	Geography	Science	The Arts
1	Mesopotamia	Maps & Globes	Planets	Cave Paintings
2	Egypt	Map Keys	Stars	Egyptian Art
3	Europe	Global Grids	Earth & Moon	Crafts
4	Ancient Greece	Wonders	Satellites	Greek Art
5	Babylon	Mapping People	Humans in Space	Poetry
6	The Levant	Physical Earth	Laws of Motion	List Poems
7	Phoenicians	Oceans	Motion	Moral Stories
8	Assyrians	Deserts	Fluids	Rhythm
9	Persians	Arctic	Waves	Melody
10	Ancient China	Forests	Machines	Chinese Art
11	Early Japan	Mountains	States of Matter	Line & Shape
12	Arabia	Rivers & Lakes	Atoms	Color & Value
13	Ancient India	Grasslands	Elements	Texture & Form
14	Ancient Africa	Africa	Bonding	African Tales
15	First North Americans	North America	Salts	Creative Kids
16	Ancient South America	South America	Plants	South American Art
17	Celts	Europe	Flowering Plants	Jewelry
18	Roman Republic	Asia	Trees	Roman Art
19	Christianity	Australia & Oceania	Simple Plants	Instruments
20	Roman Empire	You Explore	Fungi	Composing Music

2	History	Geography	Science	The Arts
1	Byzantines	Turkey	Climate & Seasons	Byzantine Art
2	Barbarians	Ireland	Forecasting	Illumination
3	Islam	Arabian Peninsula	Clouds & Precipitation	Creative Kids
4	Vikings	Norway	Special Effects	Viking Art
5	Anglo Saxons	Britain	Wild Weather	King Arthur Tales
6	Charlemagne	France	Cells and DNA	Carolingian Art
7	Normans	Nigeria	Skeletons	Canterbury Tales
8	Feudal System	Germany	Muscles, Skin, & Cardiopulmonary	Gothic Art
9	Crusades	Balkans	Digestive & Senses	Religious Art
10	Burgundy, Venice, Spain	Switzerland	Nerves	Oil Paints
11	Wars of the Roses	Russia	Health	Minstrels & Plays
12	Eastern Europe	Hungary	Metals	Printmaking
13	African Kingdoms	Mali	Carbon Chem	Textiles
14	Asian Kingdoms	Southeast Asia	Non-metals	Vivid Language
15	Mongols	Caucasus	Gases	Fun With Poetry
16	Medieval China & Japan	China	Electricity	Asian Arts
17	Pacific Peoples	Micronesia	Circuits	Arts of the Islands
18	American Peoples	Canada	Technology	Indian Legends
19	The Renaissance	Italy	Magnetism	Renaissance Art I
20	Explorers	Caribbean Sea	Motors	Renaissance Art II

3	History	Geography	Science	The Arts
1	Age of Exploration	Argentina and Chile	Classification & Insects	Fairy Tales
2	The Ottoman Empire	Egypt and Libya	Reptiles & Amphibians	Poetry
3	Mogul Empire	Pakistan & Afghanistan	Fish	Mogul Arts
4	Reformation	Angola & Zambia	Birds	Reformation Art
5	Renaissance England	Tanzania & Kenya	Mammals & Primates	Shakespeare
6	Thirty Years' War	Spain	Sound	Baroque Music
7	The Dutch	Netherlands	Light & Optics	Baroque Art I
8	France	Indonesia	Bending Light	Baroque Art II
9	The Enlightenment	Korean Pen.	Color	Art Journaling
10	Russia & Prussia	Central Asia	History of Science	Watercolors
11	Conquistadors	Baltic States	Igneous Rocks	Creative Kids
12	Settlers	Peru & Bolivia	Sedimentary Rocks	Native American Art
13	13 Colonies	Central America	Metamorphic Rocks	Settler Sayings
14	Slave Trade	Brazil	Gems & Minerals	Colonial Art
15	The South Pacific	Australasia	Fossils	Principles of Art
16	The British in India	India	Chemical Reactions	Classical Music
17	Boston Tea Party	Japan	Reversible Reactions	Folk Music
18	Founding Fathers	Iran	Compounds & Solutions	Rococo
19	Declaring Independence	Samoa and Tonga	Oxidation & Reduction	Creative Crafts I
20	The American Revolution	South Africa	Acids & Bases	Creative Crafts II

4	History	Geography	Science	The Arts
1	American Government	USA	Heat & Temperature	Patriotic Music
2	Expanding Nation	Pacific States	Motors & Engines	Tall Tales
3	Industrial Revolution	U.S. Landscapes	Energy	Romantic Art I
4	Revolutions	Mountain West States	Energy Sources	Romantic Art II
5	Africa	U.S. Political Maps	Energy Conversion	Impressionism I
6	The West	Southwest States	Earth Structure	Impressionism II
7	Civil War	National Parks	Plate Tectonics	Post-Impressionism
8	World War I	Plains States	Earthquakes	Expressionism
9	Totalitarianism	U.S. Economics	Volcanoes	Abstract Art
10	Great Depression	Heartland States	Mountain Building	Kinds of Art
11	World War II	Symbols and Landmarks	Chemistry of Air & Water	War Art
12	Modern East Asia	The South States	Food Chemistry	Modern Art
13	India's Independence	People of America	Industry	Pop Art
14	Israel	Appalachian States	Chemistry of Farming	Modern Music
15	Cold War	U.S. Territories	Chemistry of Medicine	Free Verse
16	Vietnam War	Atlantic States	Food Chains	Photography
17	Latin America	New England States	Animal Groups	Latin American Art
18	Civil Rights	Home State Study	Instincts	Theater & Film
19	Technology	Home State Study II	Habitats	Architecture
20	Terrorism	America in Review	Conservation	Creative Kids

Unit 1-11
Printable Pack

This unit includes printables at the end. To make life easier for you we also created digital printable packs for each unit. To retrieve your printable pack for Unit 1-11, please visit

www.layers-of-learning.com/digital-printable-packs/

Put the printable pack in your shopping cart and use this coupon code:

0104UNIT1-11

Your printable pack will be free.

LAYERS OF LEARNING INTRODUCTION

This is part of a series of units in the Layers of Learning homeschool curriculum, including the subjects of history, geography, science, and the arts. Children from 1st through 12th can participate in the same curriculum at the same time -f amily school style.

The units are intended to be used in order as the basis of a complete curriculum (once you add in a systematic math, reading, and writing program). You begin with Year 1 Unit 1 no matter what ages your children are. Spend about 2 weeks on each unit. You pick and choose the activities within the unit that appeal to you and read the books from the book list that are available to you or find others on the same topic from your library. We highly recommend that you use the timeline in every history section as the backbone. Then flesh out your learning with reading and activities that highlight the topics you think are the most important.

Alternatively, you can use the units as activity ideas to supplement another curriculum in any order you wish. You can still use them with all ages of children at the same time.

When you've finished with Year One, move on to Year Two, Year Three, and Year Four. Then begin again with Year One and work your way through the years again. Now your children will be older, reading more involved books, and writing more in depth. When you have completed the sequence for the second time, you start again on it for the third and final time. If your student began with Layers of Learning in 1st grade and stayed with it all the way through she would go through the four year rotation three times, firmly cementing the information in her mind in ever increasing depth. At each level you should expect increasing amounts of outside reading and writing. High schoolers in particular should be reading extensively, and if possible, participating in discussion groups.

☺ ☻ ☻ These icons will guide you in spotting activities and books that are appropriate for the age of child you are working with. But if you think an activity is too juvenile or too difficult for your kids, adjust accordingly. The icons are not there as rules, just guides.

☺ GRADES 1-4
☻ GRADES 5-8
☻ GRADES 9-12

Within each unit we share:
- EXPLORATIONS, activities relating to the topic;
- EXPERIMENTS, usually associated with science topics;
- EXPEDITIONS, field trips;
- EXPLANATIONS, teacher helps or educational philosophies.

In the sidebars we also include Additional Layers, Famous Folks, Fabulous Facts, On the Web, and other extra related topics that can take you off on tangents, exploring the world and your interests with a bit more freedom. The curriculum will always be there to pull you back on track when you're ready.

You can learn more about how to use this curriculum at www.layers-of-learning.com/layers-of-learning-program/

UNIT ELEVEN
EARLY JAPAN – MOUNTAINS – STATES OF MATTER – LINE & SHAPE

Medicine For The Soul

-Inscription over the door of the Library at Thebes

	LIBRARY LIST:
HISTORY	Search for: Ancient Japan, Jomon period, Yamato. This topic is difficult to find. You'll find loads about samurai and medieval Japan, but not much about the early stuff. ☺ ☻ Japanese Fairy Tales by Yei Theodora Ozaki. Not entirely true to the original Japanese tales, but definitely worthwhile for kids and parents to read together. ☺ ☻ Exploration Into Japan by Richard Tames. Comprehensive history of Japan from Jomon period to modern times. ☻ Ancient Jomon of Japan by Junko Habu. Readable and interesting details about the archeology that discovered the Jomon people. ☻ Prehistoric Japan: New Perspectives On Insular East Asia by Keiji Imamura. Focuses on the Jomon Period and then goes into the Yamato Period.
GEOGRAPHY	Search for: mountains, mountaineering, Everest, mountain ranges ☺ The Rocky Mountains by Marion Dane Bauer. An easy-reader, this book tells in very simple language about the largest mountain range in North America. ☺ When I Was Young in the Mountains by Cynthia Rylant. Autobiographical account of a young girl growing up in the Appalachian Mountains. ☺ About Habitats: Mountains by Cathryn Sill. Focuses on animals that live in the mountains. Your kids will love the illustrations. ☺ To the Top! Climbing the World's Highest Mountain by Sydelle Kramer. An easy reader, this is the story of the first successful ascent of Everest. ☺ ☻ I Wonder Why Mountains Have Snow on Top by Jackie Gaff. Covers just about every aspect of mountains from human uses to geology. ☺ ☻ Mountains by Seymour Simon. ☺ ☻ Mountains from Space: Peaks and Ranges of the Seven Continents by Stefan Dech, Rudiger Glasser, Reinhold Messner, Ralf-Peter Märtin. A book of satellite photographs from space of the world's mountain ranges. ☺ ☻ Within Reach: My Everest Story by Mark Pfetzer and Jack Galvin. True story about teenage mountaineer, Mark Pfetzer.

SCIENCE	Search for: matter, solids, liquids, gases ☺ <u>What Is the World Made Of? All About Solids, Liquids, and Gases</u> by Kathleen Weidner Zoehfeld and Paul Meisel. ☺ <u>What's the Matter in Mr. Whiskers' Room?</u> by Michael Elsohn Ross, Paul Meisel. Students learn about matter as they go around to the classroom science stations with their teacher. ☺ ☻ <u>Matter</u> (DK Eyewitness) by Christopher Cooper. ☺ <u>Basher Science: Physics: Why Matter Matters!</u> By Dan Green and Simon Basher. Anthropomorphic figures take your kid entertainingly through difficult concepts. ☻ <u>The Skeptical Chemist</u> by Robert Boyle. ☻ <u>Elements of Chemistry</u> by Antoine Lavoisier.
THE ARTS	Search for: art concepts, line, shape, art elements ☺ <u>Lines that Wiggle</u> by Candace Whitman. Uses rhyme and a twisting, snaking, swaying glittery line to teach art concepts about how lines move. ☺ <u>The Pencil</u> by Allan Ahlberg. A pencil goes crazy and begins to draw. Point out the lines and shapes the pencil draws as you read the book together. ☺ <u>What is Line?</u> by Susan Markowitz-Meedith. ☺ <u>What is Shape?</u> by Tea Benduhn. ☺ <u>Harold and the Purple Crayon</u> by Crockett Johnson. Classic children's storybook that uses simple lines to tell a story. ☺ ☻ <u>Lines</u> by Philip Yenawine. Uses 20th century art to teach kids about line in art. ☺ ☻ <u>Shapes</u> by Philip Yenawine. Part of the same series as <u>Lines</u>.

HISTORY: EARLY JAPAN

We know less about the early people of Japan than we do about the early Chinese because the Chinese developed writing centuries before the Japanese. Like northern Europe, Japan's written record doesn't even begin until the early Middle Ages. Historians think the people of Japan were hunter gatherers for much longer than most other people because the islands of Japan were so abundant in berries, fish, shellfish, and animals. Because of the abundance of food, the people had no need to farm for a very long time. Perhaps historians are right, but there is no real way to tell for sure, and archaeological dating is an educated guess at best. In any case, this time period in Japan that we know so little about it called the Jomon Period.

After the Jomon Period new settlers from Asia moved in and brought new crops like rice and also metalworking skills. People began to organize into tribes and had chieftains over them. Around 300 AD the Yamato tribe became especially strong, taking over several neighboring tribes. The Yamatos were the beginning of the centralized imperial government. As the ancient times ended though, the Japanese were still mostly tribal and living in small villages rather than being a part of large cities with complex governments.

☺ ☺ ☻ **EXPLORATION: Early Japan Timeline**
You will find printable timeline squares at the end of this unit.
- 14000 - 300 BC Jomon period
- 660 BC The Mythical Emperor Jimmu, a descendant of the Sun Goddess, founds the royal dynasty
- 300 BC - 250 AD Yayoi Period; weaving, rice farming, and working in iron and bronze begin
- 57 AD Japan first mentioned in Chinese records
- 220 AD Queen Himiko is chosen to bring peace to the warring Wa (Japanese) tribes, uniting them for the first time
- 250 AD - 538 AD Kofun Period; strong military states emerge
- 538 AD Buddhism is introduced to Japan by this date
- 538 - 710 AD Asuka Period; the Yamato unite and rule most of Japan
- 594 AD Prince Shotoku rules for Empress Suiko and works to spread Chinese religion and culture
- 710 AD the capital is moved from Asuka to Nara and the Nara Period begins; the empire become centralized; the emperor becomes a figurehead

☺ ☺ ☻ EXPLORATION: Shinto Creation Story

Across many cultures there are similar stories that tell about the creation of the earth. The Japanese story begins like so: "Of old, Heaven and Earth were not yet separated, and the In and Yo not yet divided. They formed a chaotic mass like an egg which was obscurely defined limits. The purer and clearer part was thinly drawn out and formed Heaven, while the heavier and grosser element settled down and became Earth. . . Heaven was therefore formed first, and Earth was established subsequently. After the creation of Heaven and Earth, Divine beings were produced between them" (condensed translation).

Compare this story to the first part of Genesis in the Bible. What similarities and differences do you notice? Why do you think so many different societies share similar stories?

Draw a picture of the images that come to your mind when hearing the Japanese creation story.

☺ ☺ ☻ EXPLORATION: Cord Pottery

"Jomon" means cord-marked. The ancient Jomon people used cords (ropes) to make designs in their pottery. It created unique and beautiful textures and designs. Making pottery was a skill that allowed them to settle in one place more easily, much like farming. They used the pots not only as decorations, but also for carrying water, as cooking vessels, and to store food and other things in. Archaeologists have found a great deal of Jomon pottery.

Make your own pot in the style of the Jomons by sculpting a bowl shape from clay or salt dough. Now wrap a small rope around a wood dowel or pencil and secure it with tape or thumb tacks on each end. While the clay pot is still soft, use the rope wrapped stick to press designs into your pot.

☺ ☻ EXPLORATION: Life in a Pit

The early Japanese didn't have fancy homes. They lived in pit homes. A pit home is just a pit dug into the ground and then covered over with something (branches or other natural materials) for protection from the weather. Imagine living in a pit in the dirt!

Famous Folks

There is an ancient Chinese tale telling of a powerful Japanese ruler who reigned for half a century, molding them into a strong and wise people. Her name was Himiko.

The legends say she was begged to take the throne after decades of upheaval, war, and unrest had been blamed on male rulers. She brought knowledge and trade goods over from China and improved the knowledge and technology of her own people.

The only thing is, not one Japanese tale of her existence can be found. The stories of this amazing ruler all come from China. Was she real or not? Was her rule purposely covered up? It's a history mystery.

Deep Readers Only

The definitive source of ancient Japanese history for English speakers is the *Cambridge History of Japan*. It's a compilation of many scholarly articles on the subject. But it's also really expensive and a bit intimidating for the layman.

Additional Layer

Learn more about Jomon art.

Photograph by Kumamushi and shared under Creative Commons license.

Choose a small toy figure, like a Lego man or a little doll, and make a pit home for your toy. Go outside to a place it's okay to dig and make a hole big enough to be a home for the toy. Find something to cover the pit with to be the roof.

Do you think it would be a nice place to live? Will it stay warm and dry in bad weather? What do you think it would be like to live there? How do you think you would get in and out?

☺ ☻ EXPLORATION: Men Versus Women

Anciently, many Japanese rulers were women. This is unusual when compared with most of the civilizations in the world, and it wasn't lasting even in Japan.

Additional Layer

Japanese food borrowed much from China over the centuries. The Japanese eat very little meat and much from the sea. Rice or noodles are the staple of every meal. Try looking up recipes and making a few Japanese dishes.

Divide a sheet of paper into two columns. Write "Women" at the top of one column and "Men" at the top of the other column. Consider the differences between men and women. Stereotypes aren't universally true, but they can be culturally revealing. List as many stereotypical qualities, both positive and negative, of each gender as you can on the paper. Circle the qualities that you believe would make a great leader. Are there qualities circled on both sides or just one column? Have a discussion about our gender roles, stereotypes, and the qualities of men and women. Talk about leadership and speculate on why men have traditionally dominated political leadership.

☺ ☻ ☻ EXPLORATION: Rice Farmer

Rice was one of the first main crops grown in Japan, and it is still grown there today. It takes about four months for a crop to grow, and the conditions have to be just right.

You can grow your own crop of rice in a bucket. Here's how:

1. Get a bucket and fill it with 6" of potting soil. Now add water until the water level is about 2 inches above the soil. Now your "field" is ready. (Some pots and buckets for plant growing have drainage holes in the bottom, but you want your bucket to be water tight because rice grows best in swampy, wet fields.)

2. Sprinkle long grain brown rice on your field. You can't use white rice because it has been processed. The rice grains will sink below the water level and rest on the top of the dirt in your bucket. Keep your rice in a nice, sunny, warm spot. Always keep the water level about 2 inches above the dirt.

3. Once your plants are about 6 inches tall add even more water. Now your field should be covered with about 4 inches of water. After that, let the water level slowly decrease as the rice grows, and when it's just about dried up your rice should be ready for harvest. You can tell it's ready when the stalks have changed from green to gold in color.

4. Harvest your stalks by cutting them down, wrapping them in newspaper, and let them dry in a warm place for 3 weeks. After 3 weeks you can take them out and roast them in a 200 degree oven for an hour. Now remove the hulls by hand. Now you can cook your rice!

It's a lot of hard work and waiting for just a little bit of rice, especially when it's one of the least expensive grains at the grocery store. Today the Japanese government subsidizes rice farmers to give them incentive to keep growing it.

☺ ☻ ❂ **EXPLORATION: A Rose By Any Other Name**

There was a time when the Japanese people had no surnames, but the government declared that everyone had to choose one. Most people chose a name that described either their job or a place nearby to their home. 3/4ths of the population were farmers, so nearly everyone lived by a rice paddy (rice field).

Because rice is such an important crop, the symbol for field 田 (pronounced "ta") literally meant rice paddy in Japanese. Still today, many Japanese names have ta in them.

Tanaka (田 中) and Nakata (中 田) mean "middle of the paddy field"
Kawada (川 田) means "paddy field by a river"
Furuta (古 田) means "old paddy field"

Additional Layer
It was Shakespeare, in *Romeo and Juliet*, who said, "What's in a name? That which we call a rose by any other name would smell as sweet."

Additional Layer
Government mandated surnames have happened in other parts of the world too. In fact, most people throughout much of the world had no name other than their given name until their government demanded it. Look up these occurrences:

Laos 1943

China 2852 BC

Netherlands 1811

Thailand 1920

England 1086

In other places there are still no family surnames, for example:

Iceland

Tibet

Java

East Africa

You might think it's strange to be named after a field, but it's not so different than our names today. My son's name is Tyler which literally means "layer of tile." I also know people named Rose, Apple, and Forrest. If you were to give yourself a name based on something near where you lived, what might it be? I might be "Raspberry" because of the raspberry patch I have in my backyard.

☺ ☻ EXPLORATION: Jimmu and The Three Treasures

Legend has it that the sun goddess, Amaterasu, looked down on Japan and saw nothing but chaos. She saw the tribes fighting with one another, the people unsettled, and unhappiness everywhere. She decided something must be done, so she sent three gifts down to the earth. She gave them to her grandson who chose Jimmu, leader of the Yamatos, to be the recipient of the 3 gifts-- a curved jewel, a sword, and a sacred mirror. With the gifts, Jimmu became the first Emperor of the Imperial Line. He founded the imperial dynasty and brought peace to Japan. The sword represents valor, the mirror represents wisdom, and the jewel represents benevolence. The treasures have been passed down from emperor to emperor and are still part of the Emperor's regalia. They are of utmost importance to the Japanese people.

The sword is rather obvious in representing valor. A ruler needs strength and bravery to keep a people safe. But what about a mirror representing wisdom? What is the meaning behind that? And a curved jade jewel representing benevolence? How is that significant? Talk about it together and see what you come up with.

How would those three gifts used wisely by a leader bring an end to the chaos, fighting, and unhappiness of the people we heard of at the beginning of the legend?

Write an end to the tale. What did Jimmu do with the three objects to bring peace?

☺ ☻ EXPLORATION: The Yamato Court and Cultural Exchange

The Japanese were not as technologically advanced as their

neighbors. They learned many things from the Chinese in particular. They learned better farming techniques, how to make iron and bronze weapons and tools, and how to make cloth. Because of the geography of Japan, the islands closest to the mainland experienced the earliest and greatest cultural exchange.

The flow of knowledge from China to Japan became more substantial during the Yamato rule. The Yamato court invited Chinese technical advisers and scholars to come and teach them all they could. They brought Chinese scripts and and works of Confucius, among other things. Japanese students were also sent to China to study and learn things that would have been unavailable to them in their own country.

Many people argue that cultural exchange can be harmful. What do you think? Is more knowledge and technology always better? Is it the same to be gifted the knowledge as it is to develop the technology on your own? What harmful effects could it have? How could cultural exchange be beneficial?

Imagine you were to encounter a remote tribe of people with very little technology, what three things would you share with them that you think would benefit them most? Write about it.

☺ ☻ EXPLORATION: Rulers Without Power

Japanese emperors had the utmost respect of their people. They were treated as gods and served as an important religious symbol. They had almost no political power at all though. The real ruler was the shogun. He was like a warlord or prime minister, and whichever shogun was the most powerful and won in battle, became the ruler. No matter how powerful the shoguns became, they never challenged the position of the emperor. The emperor was thought to possess magical powers and be able to converse with heaven for his people. Which job would you rather have – emperor or shogun?

Do some research. Are there other countries that have two leaders, one with ruling power and the other as a figurehead or spiritual ruler? Make a list of some that you find.

☺ ☻ EXPLORATION: Piggybacking Down the Kaido

Japan had been quite divided with small isolated towns for many years, but began to develop a system of roads, called kaido, to the capital city of Kyoto. There were seven kaido constructed so that travel and trade with the capital would be easier. Although they wanted the convenience, they were leery about creating roads that enemies could too easily use to get to the capital. Because of

Additional Layer

Climate change may have played a role in the history of the Jomon people. During their early years (4000-2000 BC) the climate was significantly warmer than the present day, causing the seas to rise and the temperature to be more mild. This meant plentiful food and a population explosion.

Then in around 1500 BC the climate cooled, sea levels dropped, and the population of the Jomon decreased sharply.

Fabulous Fact

It appears that all through their history, even when populations were high and the people were sedentary, the Jomon lived a hunter-gatherer lifestyle. Though there is also some evidence they had kitchen gardens of millet, gourds, and vegetables.

Additional Layer

When we talk about the earliest history of the Americas we talk about people migrating in to the continent. Many people believe the Jomon were some of those who did the migrating.

Fabulous Fact

The Kaido system of roads was expanded and revised during the medieval ages in Japan and the the center of the road system was at Edo (Tokyo), which was the new capital.

Many modern roads follow these ancient routes.

From the woodcut print series *The Fifty-three Stations of Tokaido* by Utagawa Hiroshige

Coloring Sheet

You'll find an ancient Japanese temple coloring sheet to accompany this unit in the printables at the end of the unit.

The Japanese have been remarkably good at preserving their old temples, shrines, and castles so there are many beautiful examples from very ancient times still standing.

this, no bridges were built on the roads to help travelers or an invading army traverse the waterways and rivers. No boats or ferries were allowed either. Instead, porters carried the people across the rivers on their shoulders or their backs.

Get in teams of two. One person will be the porter and one will be the traveler. The traveler needs a backpack with items he's transporting in it. If you want to be authentic you can put salt and fish in the backpack. One kaido was called the Salt Way and was used for transporting salt and seafood from the Sea of Japan. The porter must let the traveler climb on his back or shoulders and cross the street 10 times. Now trade places and let the traveler try out the hard job of the porter. Now imagine that you aren't crossing a street; you are crossing a flowing river. You have to do it over and over again when a traveler wants to cross.

☺ ☺ ☻ **EXPLORATION: Map of the Yamato**

At the end of this unit you will find a map of Ancient Japan to color. It shows the Nara kingdom and some of the major highways.

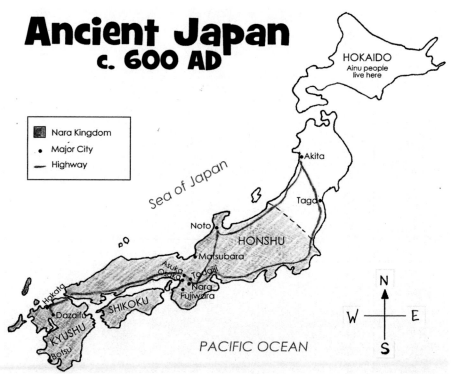

GEOGRAPHY: MOUNTAINS

Mountains are beautiful, hostile, barriers flung across continents. They stop the progress of armies, pioneers, and the rain. They create weather all their own as air rises up their sides. They create islands of life, stranded in specialized zones on their slopes. Mountains represent a challenge to be conquered and a force to be respected.

Hochsgelau by Hubert Landa, c. 1900

Mountains can be formed and classified as one of four types:
- Volcanic
- Dome
- Fault-Block
- Fold

Volcanic Mountain

Fold Mountain

Fault-Block

Fabulous Fact

The study of mountains is called orography.

The study of mountains on other planets is called exogeology.

Fabulous Fact

The top 100 highest mountains in the world are all in Asia; in the Himalayas, Hindu Kush, and Karakorum ranges. Here is Mt. Everest – the tallest mountain in the world. Make a list of at least the top ten.

In this unit we'll learn about landforms associated with mountains, where they are in the world, human activities surrounding mountains, and how they affect the land around them.

☺ ☻ ☻ **EXPLORATION: Mapping Mountains**
Make a map of the major mountain ranges of the world. Once you've made the map, memorize the names and locations of the major mountain ranges by practicing pointing them out on a world map when someone calls out the names.

To make your map, use the world map from the end of this unit and a student atlas. Draw in the mountains. Include these mountains and for older kids, also include these mountain peaks:

Additional Layer

Why is it colder on top of a mountain than at its base?

Air acts as a blanket over the earth, trapping in the heat that radiates to the ground or water from the sun. This is what we call the greenhouse effect.

But higher in the atmosphere there is less air. Less air means a thinner blanket and more heat gets out.

Fabulous Fact

Many mountains in the western United States bear the letters of their local school on their bare slopes.

Fabulous Fact

Gannett Peak, Wind River Range, Wyoming, USA.

See if you can find it on a map of Wyoming.

Mountain Ranges

Alps
Zagros
Himalayas
Atlas
Andes
Urals
Carpathians
Rockies
Appalachian
Sierra Madre
Drakensberg
Balkans
Caucasus
Hindu Kush
Western Ghats
Eastern Ghats
Altai
Great Dividing Range

Mountain Peaks

Mount McKinley
Cerro Aconcagua
Kilimanjaro
Mont Blanc
El'brus
Mount Everest
Aoraki

Mt. McKinley

☺ ☻ EXPLORATION: Mineral Map

Make a mineral map of the United States. Use the Mineral Map from the end of this unit. The minerals and precious metals are marked on the map and there is a key. Color the minerals and the key. Notice that most mineral deposits are in mountains. Why do you think this is so?

☺ ☻ EXPLORATION: Mountain Range Model

Using salt dough, make a model of a mountain range. You can use a real place on Earth like the Carpathian Mountains, the Alps, the Rocky Mountains, or the Andes Mountains, or you can let your student make up an imaginary land. Build your 3-D map model on a cardboard base. Include passes, glaciers, peaks, ridges, hills and foothills in your design. You can also add in streams and waterfalls if you'd like. After it is dry, you can paint and label it. If you'd prefer, you can make labeled flags with small papers glued to toothpicks. Stick them into the wet dough before it dries.

Salt Dough
2 c. flour
1 c. salt
½ c. water
1 t. cooking oil

Just mix the salt and flour then add in the oil and water. Mix thoroughly. Food coloring can be added if you'd like. Let dry for several days to make it permanent or keep it in a sealed bag in the fridge for three to four weeks.

☻ EXPLORATION: Mountainscape

Using a large lump of salt dough, form a large mountain peak. Mark the peak with a dot with the tip of a toothpick. Using the toothpick, draw a line from "north" to "south" across the mountain, and another perpendicular line running from "east" to "west." You've just drawn orientation lines. Now you will draw three rings around your center dot. The first ring goes a quarter of the way down your mountain, the second goes halfway down, and the third goes three quarters of the way down.

Next, use a piece of fishing line or tough thread, pull it tight, and use it to slice through your clay mountain along the lines you just drew. You'll have four layers. Place the bottom layer on a piece of paper and trace it, making sure to record where the orientation lines are. Remove it, and do it again with the next layers, one at a time. You'll have to use the orientation lines to make sure your mountain diagram is aligned properly.

Once your lines are all drawn, you'll finish your map by coloring each elevation layer and creating a key to show the elevations. Add more details.

☺ ☻ EXPLORATION: Mountain Landforms

Learn some of the landforms associated with mountainous areas.

Mountain: An upthrust of rock, high above the surrounding land
Peak: The topmost projection of a mountain, also called the summit, crest, or pinnacle
Ridge: the upper edge of a chain of mountains
Glacier: A mass of ice the builds on the upper slopes of a mountain and then slowly slides down
Range: A connected chain of mountains
Continental Divide: A long ridge line of mountains that determines the direction a continent's rivers flow
Mountain Pass: A path through the mountains between peaks
Valley: A low depression between hills or mountains
Volcano: An opening in the earth's crust where lava flows out, often creating a mountain of new rock

Once you've reviewed or learned the definitions, make a batch of crispy rice treats. Let it cool slightly. Then give each child a portion on a paper plate. Have them shape the crispy treats into mountain shapes, trying to add in as many of the mountain landforms as possible.

Give each child a turn to explain the landforms they used.

Additional Layer
Books where mountains figure big:
Heidi
Banner in the Sky
My Side of the Mountain
The Hobbit

Additional Layer
Mountains have often been held sacred to various people, because they are high, nearer heaven, inaccessible, and mostly uninhabited.

Mount Shasta, USA: sacred to Native Americans

Mount Fuji, Japan: Sacred to the Shinto religion

Mauna Kea, Hawaii: sacred to the native Hawaiian religion

Mount Sinai, Egypt: sacred to Jews and Christians

Song Shan, China: sacred to Taoists

Mount Kailash, Tibet: sacred to Hindus, Buddhists, Jains, and Bons

Mount Tabor, Israel: sacred to Christians

Writer's Workshop

Write a research report on mountains. Have the kids find three facts on mountains. For younger kids, their report should just be one paragraph, with an introductory sentence, one sentence for each fact, and a conclusion sentence.

Older kids can expand their five sentences into five paragraphs.

You can find a printable report organizer for young kids and intermediate writers in the printables at www.Layers-of-Learning.com.

On The Web

What kind of gear do you need to climb a frozen wasteland that is the top of a high mountain peak?

Find out here: http://www.pbs.org/wgbh/nova/tech/outfitting-ice-climber.html

Here you'll find an incredible panoramic photo of the view from Everest: http://www.panoramas.dk/fullscreen2/full22.html

And don't miss this little gem of a film on the Canadian Rockies: http://youtu.be/wnPQ2XT8Qvw

Crispy Rice Recipe (makes enough for 2-3 kids)
 ½ c. butter or margarine
1 12 oz bag of marshmallows
6 cups crisp rice cereal

Melt the butter in a saucepan. Add marshmallows and stir until melted. Pour over the crisp rice cereal in a large bowl. Stir well.

*Tip: wet your hands with cold water to keep the warm marshmallow from sticking all over your hands.

☻ ☻ EXPLORATION: Ski Resorts

Ski resorts can be found all over the world. Find these resorts using an atlas. Plot them on a world map then choose one to make a travel brochure about. You can find a printable travel brochure on Layers of Learning at http://www.layers-of-learning.com/travel-brochure/.

> Sun Valley, Idaho, USA
> Andorra
> Las Lenas, Argentina
> Sugar Loaf, Maine, USA
> Banff, Alberta, Canada
> Mont Tremblant, Quebec, Canada
> Innsbruck, Austria
> Chamonix, France
> Telluride, Colorado, USA
> Park City, Utah, USA
> Grindelwald, Switzerland
> St. Moritz, Switzerland
> Valle Nevado, Chili
> Lake Placid, New York, USA

☻ EXPLORATION: Animals of the Mountains

Animals that live on mountain sides are able to deal with the cold temperatures, short summers, and low oxygen of the heights.

For this craft you'll need a copy of the worksheet at the end of this unit, a paper plate, a metal paper fastener, scissors, and crayons or markers.

Choose one or several animals that you want to use in the craft. Cut out your animals. Color your animals and glue it onto stiff paper or thin cardboard. Next color your paper plate to look like a mountain. The upper half will be the peak with a treeline, alpine fields, tundra, and an ice covered peak. The lower half of the plate should be a coniferous forest.

Next fasten the paper brad through the front of the plate and then through the stem of your animal's paper. Now your animal can climb up and down the mountain.

You could assign the student a report to write about their animal as well if you like. Have them answer these questions: Where does it live? What does it eat? What does it do in the winter? If the student comes across other information they may include that as well.

☺ ☺ ☻ EXPLORATION: Life in the Mountains

People who live in the mountains have to adapt to the mountain climate and weather. The biggest difference is that they may have to deal with heavier snowfalls and shorter growing seasons. Life isn't so different for someone who lives in the Rocky Mountains of North America, accessible to modern conveniences, but in many mountainous areas of the world their lives are quite different.

Choose a mountainous country like Nepal, Peru, Bolivia, Switzerland, or Bhutan. Learn about the people who live in the mountains of these countries. Pay special attention to how they have adapted their lifestyle and their homes to the environment of the mountains. Make a poster showing pictures of what you have learned along with captions.

☺ ☻ EXPLORATION: Mountaineering

Going places no one has ever set foot has often been the goal of adventurous human beings, especially since the days of Henry the Navigator and the Age of Exploration. Reaching the summit of a high or difficult mountain is one of the greatest and most dangerous trips people have ever taken.

Learn about the conquering

Additional Layer

The stories of mountaineers and the hardships they faced, even losing their lives in many cases, is a great entry into talking about moral values. Here are some things to think about with your kids.

What is the value of setting a worthwhile goal?

Do you feel better when you achieve something easy or something difficult?

Is climbing a mountain something you can buy or something that can be given to you? What else cannot be given? Would you want these things to just be given to you? Would you value them as much if they were?

What did the mountaineers have to do to prepare for their climbs? What do you have to do to reach a difficult goal?

Excerpt from a poem by J.R.R. Tolkien (The Hobbit)

Far over the Misty Mountains cold,
To dungeons deep and caverns old,
We must away, ere break of day,
To seek our pale enchanted gold.

Explanation

Whatever your religious tradition, you should spend some formal time teaching it to your kids. Whether you have them read your holy words or meditate or pray is up to you, but there is great value in taking care of the spiritual.

This is an area that schools will not and should not enter into, so parents need to do more, even if the Sunday school is teaching your kids. Parents have huge influence and the lessons taught at home by the people who love them most are the ones that will have the most impact.

Michelle

Fabulous Fact

These are the beautiful table mountains of Venezuela:

Find Venezuela on a world map.

of Mount Everest or another mountain and the dangers of high altitude trips.

This video shows a 2008 climbing expedition of K2. http://youtu.be/HgVryHjBmxY. During the descent the expedition leader became lost and was stranded for three days. During his rescue another member of the team lost his life.

Why do people want to go into the unknown? How have these trips changed over the years? Has it gotten easier, harder, stayed the same? Why?

Plan a mountaineering trip. What special equipment would you need? Who would you take with you? What season of the year would be best to go? How would you travel to the base camp starting point? Write up your plan and find as much information as you can about the mountain and the expedition.

☺ ☺ ☻ EXPEDITION: Go Climb a Mountain

Plan a trip to a mountain near you. Pick an easily climbed one with a well-worn trail to begin. Plan your trip, and prepare for it by doing several shorter hikes first. Don't forget water, food, and an emergency kit. It's extremely unlikely you'll have cell phone coverage so be sure someone knows where you are and when you'll be back. Even well-worn trails on familiar mountains can be dangerous if a storm comes up, if the hike takes longer than you expect and dark settles in, or if someone sustains even a minor injury. Even experienced mountaineers on well-known hikes in the summer have come to great grief. Be careful. You may wish to climb only part of the way up the mountain, depending on your readiness and the ages of your children.

If an actual hike is out of the question, take a trip to the top on a ski lift. Most ski resorts have their lifts run all summer for sightseers, hikers, and mountain bikers.

☺ ☻ EXPLORATION: Life Zones

As you ascend up a mountain the conditions of temperature and moisture change and so do the plants and animals that can live in these conditions. We call these different conditions life zones.

Make a book of the various life zones on a mountain slope. First, lay eight sheets of paper on top of each other. Draw a mountain shape on the top paper. Then, with all the sheets together cut out the mountain shape. The top sheet is the cover. Give it the title "Mountain Zones." We'll use an imaginary mountain in the Himalayas for our example. The remaining pages will be labeled as such in this order from the base of the mountain to the summit:

1. Warm deciduous forest
2. Temperate deciduous forest
3. Cool coniferous forest
4. Low-growing shrubs
5. Alpine grassland
6. Tundra
7. Snow and rock

Himalayan Mountain Zones

Each page will have an illustration in the appropriate place on the mountain to show that terrain type. Include a caption about the plants and animals that would be found in this zone. Here's a little help:

1. Warm deciduous forest: a sub-tropical jungle with sal, arjun, and teak trees. Himalayan langur monkeys move up and down the mountain with the seasons.
2. Temperate deciduous forest: oak and rhododendron trees
3. Cool coniferous forest: cedar, pine, fur trees. Red pandas, which look something like a raccoon, live here.
4. Low-growing shrubs: rhododendron, dwarf birch, juniper bushes
5. Alpine grassland: grass, low-growing flowers, rodents, and insects. Wild ass, takins (like an ox), and snow leopards live here in the summer, moving down the mountain in winter.
6. Tundra: bare rock and perpetually frozen soil.
7. Snow and rock: at the summit, nothing lives, but the

Additional Layer

A view from space of the Chilean Andes. You can see glaciers and the paths they leave behind.

Photograph by NASA

Additional Layer

"I Love Mountains" is an interactive book by Sloan Graham in an app for the iPad and iPhone. Very highly recommended!

Additional Layer

The largest mountains and mountain ranges in the world are in the sea, not on land. If you measure from the level plain a mountain sits on, the tallest mountain on Earth is actually Mauna Kea, the Big Island of Hawaii. Most of it is underwater, so it doesn't seem all that high from our vantage point. The biggest mountain in the solar system is Olympus Mons on Mars.

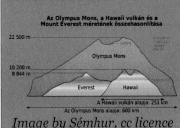

Image by Sémhur, cc licence

Additional Layer

Japan sits right along the ring of fire, an area of volcanic and earthquake activity due to movement of the earth's plates. A study of the ring of fire or plate tectonics would fit right in.

Teaching Tip

Every now and then you need to step back and re-evaluate your approach to teaching your kids.

Remember what is most important. What are your priorities? Are your goals being met?

Some things to keep in mind:

The most important thing to teach your kids is good values and morals.

The second most important thing is how to work and be self-motivated.

The third thing is how to learn, including the tools of reading, writing and mathematics.

And a distant fourth is filling their heads with awesome facts about the world.

Lammergeier, a type of vulture, may fly this high on rising warm air currents.

EXPLANATION: Depth vs. Breadth

DEPTH, INTEREST, and EXCITEMENT are much more key to a child's education than ensuring that every point is covered perfectly. When I plan my lessons, I research my overall subjects until I find something that I think the kids will find wildly interesting, and then I take off from there . . .

This week I found something wildly interesting about mountains and Japanese geography. Japan is mostly mountains, about 70 percent in fact. Most of its mountains are volcanoes. There is a monkey called the Japanese Macaque monkey that lives in the colder, snowy parts of these volcanic mountains. They soak in the warm volcanic mountain springs.

That's my kind of monkey! Makes me want to go out and buy a hot tub . . . do you think that would qualify as an educational expense? We got online and read up a little on these guys, looked at a lot of great pictures, and are using them as our jumping off point for other projects.

SCIENCE: STATES OF MATTER

Matter is the word for all the stuff in the universe. It makes up everything, from the furniture in your house to your body to the air that you breathe. Everything is made up of matter. Because we like to organize and define things, humans have put matter into categories. There are four broad categories of matter: solids, liquids, gases, and plasma. Matter can change from one of these states to another. Beyond this, each individual type of matter has certain properties that are unique to it. For example, plastic does not conduct electricity; it is solid at normal temperatures on Earth; it is insoluble in water and easy to melt at a low temperature. Also, when it is a liquid it is easily molded into any desired shape, and will retain that shape as it solidifies. It burns, but not very well, and it is very strong for its mass. These specific properties make plastics suitable for some uses, but not others. Plastics make excellent bicycle helmets because they are strong, light and easily molded, but a plastic stove top would be disastrous.

☺ EXPERIMENT: Frying Ice
You can easily show young children the three (most common) states of matter by doing a simple demonstration.

Get a frying pan hot, and then have the kids drop ice cubes into the pan. The solid ice melts to a liquid and then evaporates as steam. (Steam is technically still a liquid, but in tiny drops. Once water is a gas you can't see it at all.)

For thousands of years people have been trying to figure out what the fundamental building blocks, or elements, of the universe are.

The ancients, beginning with Aristotle, thought the basic elements were earth, air, water, and fire. They also believed that one element might be changed to another. This gave rise to alchemy, which, once the old thought shackles of the four mutable elements were thrown off, led to chemistry.

It wasn't until 1649 and the discovery of phosphorus (discovered by boiling down gallons of urine for days and days while in the pursuit of the philosopher's stone – sounds like a novel) that people began to question the old four element theory.

Molecules and atoms were discovered later.

But whatever people's philosophies have been, they've always suspected that the universe is made of something fundamental, something simple and elegant.

We still haven't really figured that one out entirely.

Additional Layer

An entire temperature scale based on water? Find out the history behind the Celsius scale.

Additional Layer

Bake a cake or brownies. What temperature do you think the brownies reach in a oven heated to 375°F? Not 375°F. That would be burning the brownies. Brownies and other baked goods are full of water. During the baking, the water is evaporating and the temperature of the brownies stays at around 212°F. Take your brownies' temperature with a candy thermometer to see just how hot they are fresh out of the oven.

Additional Layer

Water is one of very few types of matter that can be found in solid, liquid, and gas states in everyday life on Earth. Make a poster showing the water cycle and how all three states of matter are important to life.

In a matter of minutes you saw water transform from a solid to a liquid to a gas.

☺ EXPERIMENT: You Can't See It, But It's Real

Gases are the toughest concept for little kids because, for the most part, you can't see them. You can show that gases are real "stuff" (or matter) by blowing up a balloon and showing how there's something inside; this is gas.

Gas also has mass. Demonstrate this by comparing the weight of an empty balloon to a full balloon. You'll need a *balance with the empty balloon on one side and the full balloon on the other. Which has more mass?

If you don't have a balance, you can make a homemade one by tying the balloons to opposite ends of a wooden dowel or a straw. Place your finger right in the center so the stick is balancing on your finger.

☺ ☺ EXPERIMENT: Freezing Cold and Boiling Hot

Different substances have different temperatures at which they melt and evaporate. Find the freezing point and boiling point of water.

1. Place a pan of ice on a stove top with a thermometer in it. You can use a scientific thermometer designed for high temperatures or a candy thermometer.
2. Turn on the heat to the stove to a medium temperature.
3. Record the temperature every 30 seconds on a table until the water has been boiling for three minutes.
4. Plot the data on a graph.

The temperatures should plateau for a few readings when you get to the melting point and the boiling point. Then the temperature will continue to climb. The melting point of water is about 0° C (32°F) and the boiling point is about 100°C (212°F), but the exact change of state temperatures will depend on the elevation the experiment is conducted at. In places with a higher elevation, the air pressure will be less, allowing the water to boil at a lower temperature.

☺ ☺ ☺ EXPERIMENT: Microwaving Plasma

There is a fourth state of matter called plasma. Plasma occurs when high amounts of electricity are present, as in the upper atmosphere during a lightning storm, or in the high heat, high energy environment of stars.

On You Tube you can find videos of a plasma experiment in the microwave. Search for "microwave plasma experiment." We can't recommend doing it at home, so this one is a virtual experiment, but it is fun to watch the video. The glow at the top of the jar is the plasma. Plasma is highly charged matter--it's matter where the atoms are going nuts.

☺ ☻ EXPEDITION: Matter Hunt

Go on a matter field trip around your house or yard and point out different objects and which type of matter they are.

☺ ☻ ☻ EXPERIMENT: Soda Pop Sublimation

Usually matter passes from solid to liquid to gas, in that order, as it heats up. This is not always true though. Some matter can pass right by the liquid stage or never reach the gas stage. For example, we've never seen a log melt before it sent smoke up as gases. Even things that usually melt don't always pass through the liquid stage before becoming gas.

Have you ever wondered why the ice cubes in your freezer shrink if not used for several months or how the snowbanks on the side of the road seem to fade away over a long winter even when the temperatures remain cold? This is called sublimation: the process of a solid turning directly into a gas. Here's another example: dry ice (solid CO_2) turns directly into a gas without ever being a liquid. Make some homemade soda pop to demonstrate this.

In a large pitcher or cooler, add 1 gallon of juice (any flavor) and 2 pounds dry ice. You can add more juice and dry ice, just keep the proportions 1 gallon to 2 pounds. Let it sit for an hour or more. The dry ice (solid carbon dioxide or CO_2) will sublimate, leaving behind carbon dioxide dissolved in the juice and giving you a fizzy drink.

Warning: DRY ICE IS EXTREMELY COLD (-78.5 degree C or -109.3 degrees F). When you're handling it you should always wear gloves or an oven mitt. Prolonged contact with your skin will freeze your cells and cause an injury very similar to a burn. Kids shouldn't handle it at all unless they are supervised and mature enough to understand the risks and avoid injury.

Additional Layer

Learn more about the plasma phenomenon known as the northern lights. Draw or paint your own depiction of the northern lights.

Additional Layer

Did you know that not all fires can be put out with water? That is because of the properties of the burning matter. If you put water on certain fires, chemical or oil, you can make things much worse. Find out what is in your family fire extinguisher and how the chemicals work with certain materials to put out the fire.

Famous Folks

In the 1600's Englishman Robert Boyle became the first scientist to practice what we now consider modern chemistry.

Portrait by Johann Kerseboom, c. 1689

Teaching Tip

Chemical reactions make for memorable science lessons. Instead of using your breath to fill up a balloon, try using this experiment.

Before beginning, stretch out the balloon so it's easier to inflate. Pour 40 mL of water into a clean, empty soft drink bottle. Add a teaspoon of baking soda and stir it around with a straw until it has dissolved. Pour the lemon juice in and quickly put the stretched balloon over the mouth of the bottle.

You'll see your balloon inflate. Adding the lemon juice to the baking soda creates a chemical reaction between the basic baking soda and the acidic lemon juice. Together, they create carbon dioxide, a gas that rises up and fills the balloon.

Tip – you can also use vinegar in place of the lemon juice.

☺ ☺ ☻ EXPLORATION: Matter and Density

Solids, liquids, and gases make a little more sense when you look at the microscopic make-up of matter. Start by taking as many kids as you can possibly get into a hula hoop, then ask them to dance, jump, and wiggle. Not too easy when all those "molecules" are packed tightly! That's like a solid.

Now have a few kids step out and ask the same thing – that's like a liquid. The particles have a little more room to move.

And finally, leave just one kid in the hula hoop and have her move it and shake it! She can move all over any way she wants . . . plenty of room when you're a gas!

The way that molecules are packed together shows how they behave. Solids are packed tightly, usually in a regular pattern. They retain a fixed shape. Liquids are close together, but not regularly arranged. They conform to the shape of whatever contained they are in. They slide, move, flow, and vibrate. Gases have plenty of room; this allows them to move freely about as they please. Unlike solids, they are also compressible because there's still plenty of room in between their molecules.

Here's another way to show this concept:

See these 3 identical clear cubes? The first one is tightly packed like a solid. If I shake it, the pom-poms inside can't move. The middle one is like a liquid. There are lots of molecules, but not so many that it can't move and flow as liquid does. And the last one is like a gas – very few molecules, all with plenty of space. When I shake this box the molecules move freely. And now you understand states of matter . . . molecularly!

Have kids draw a picture of this concept and then write examples of lots of solids, liquids, and gases to help *solidify* the concept. *(I couldn't help myself!)*

☺ ☺ ☻ EXPERIMENT: Properties of Matter

Different types of matter have different properties. For example, water freezes at 0 deg C or 32 deg F, but oil does not. They have different properties and it is those properties that make them useful for a variety of needs. Plastic is very useful in making bicycle helmets because of its ability to be molded into any shape and retain that shape upon cooling. Plastic is durable and lightweight. A wooden helmet would not work so well, however. Wood cannot be melted and poured into a shape. Wood must be carved, and once it was, it would be very heavy and not flexible enough to absorb the impact of an accident. So we use plastic for helmets and wood for building houses.

Gather several different types of materials and make a table of some of the properties they possess. Include some or all of the following: heat conductivity, melting point, boiling point, solubility in water (can it dissolve in water?), elasticity (Can it stretch?), malleability (Can it be pounded into a shape without breaking it?), electrical conductivity, and natural state at room temperature. You may need to experiment or research on the internet to find some of the information.

Review

To review what you've learned about the states of matter during this unit, make a foldable.

Start by drawing a line about one inch from the top of the line side of the paper, then fold the piece of paper lengthwise to line up with your drawn line.

Divide it into 4 sections and cut down only the front side. This will create small flaps for each section. Write "Matter" at the top, then label each door with a state of matter. Flip open the doors to write what you've learned about each state.

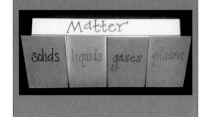

Here's an example of a table:

	State of Matter	Heat Conductivity	Melting Point	Boiling Point or Flash Point	Solubility	Elasticity	Malleability
Water	liquid	high	32 deg F	212 deg F	NA	none	none
Table salt	solid	low	800 deg F	NA	high	none	none
Wood	solid	low	NA	572 deg F	none	none	none
Cotton Fabric	solid	low	NA	250 deg F	none	medium	none
Latex Balloon	solid	low	250 deg	?	none	high	none
Copper Penny	solid	high	1981 deg F	4652 deg F	none	none	high
Cooking Oil	liquid	high	?	320 deg F	none	none	None
Oxygen	gas	high	-361 deg F	-297 deg F	low	none	none

THE ARTS: LINE AND SHAPE

Technical Art Skills

Fewer and fewer artists go to the effort of learning great technical skills and mastery of their medium. Their art is not about making a realistic representation, it's about sending a message or showing off their philosophies. The height of technical art skills was reached in the 1400's with the great Dutch oil painters. (But that's just my opinion; and if there's anything art is full of, it's opinion.)

Detail from "Man With A Turban" by Jan Van Eyke

Explanation

The more you know about art, the more you appreciate it. In other words, you really can't teach "art appreciation." You can't make someone like art, but you can expose your kids to lots of art and teach them to have a trained eye when they look at it. They will naturally find their favorites and appreciate art all on their own.

Line and shape are two of the basic elements of art. They are tools that artists use to create art. We can use these elements when <u>creating art</u> to be better artists, and we can also use them when <u>looking at art</u> so we can view it with a more understanding and a critical eye.

Lines seem simple, but they accomplish a lot. Lines are the building blocks. They are one dimensional and can be various widths, lengths, and directions. They can be horizontal, vertical, or diagonal. They can be straight or curved, thick or thin, all alone or combined with many other lines. Sometimes they are used simply to define the edges of a form. Other times they can do much more, like communicate emotion, help unify a piece of art, or convey movement. Sometimes they are actually there, and other times they are just implied. This painting is called *The Pieta* by Giotto. What does the diagonal line running along the wall of this painting do? If you aren't sure, do several of the explorations below, and then return to the painting and see if you have some answers.

Shape, like line, can define objects in space. Shapes have two dimensions — height and width. They have to be enclosed to be a shape. Unconnected lines aren't shapes; they are just lines. Shapes can be geometric (like squares, rectangles, circles, diamonds, and other shapes you can name) or organic (any enclosed shape that doesn't necessarily have a name); they are often irregular or asymmetrical. Typically things that are man made tend to have geometric shapes (look around at the furniture in your house and you'll probably see what I mean), and things that occur naturally (like animals, trees, clouds, and rivers) are organic shapes. The placement and repetition of shapes also gives clues about what is important in a piece and which objects are closer and further away. Shapes can be used to create patterns and textures too.

Which shapes are geometric and which are organic?

⊙ ☻ ☻ **EXPLORATION: The Feeling of Lines**

Lines can show feelings and communicate ideas.

Horizontal lines are usually restful because when something is parallel to the ground it feels like it is at rest to us. They feel calming and communicate relaxation. Landscape paintings often have horizontal lines.

Vertical lines communicate strength, alertness, dignity, order, and formality. They also help give height to a piece.

Diagonal lines suggest energy, movement, emotion, and passion.

Giotto di Bondone (c. 1267 - 1337) is the father of modern painting.

Additional Layer

When animated or computer graphic motion picture artists create the emotions and movements of a character, they study the movements and emotions of real live actors and copy the lines they see in their bodies and faces.

Memorization Station

As you come across artists and their art, keep a file of some of the art pieces. You can make photo copies from art books, print images off the internet or buy art postcards. Every now and then get out the cards and review the artists and pieces of art until the kids can identify the artist, the movement and the title of the art work. Give them points or prizes for correct answers.

This is one step toward making your children culturally literate and truly well educated.

Curved lines suggest grace and beauty, spontaneity and playfulness, romance and music.

Jagged lines are thought of as pain, difficulty, and trouble.

Broken lines are associated with insecurity and tentativeness.

Start by making a list of some feelings that we have (angry, happy, sad, scared, lonely, excited, and so on). Each kid can choose one of the emotions from the list. Using a white sheet of paper (or your sketchbook) and a pencil or a thin, black marker, fill your page up with lines that communicate that emotion. It may take some practice. A downward spiral may feel sad, various sizes of round circles may feel playful, jagged lines might feel angry. Try some out and see if you can convey the emotion you wanted to.

☺ ☺ ☻ EXPLORATION: Line Sampler

Take a blank sheet of paper and divide it into 16 squares (just draw 4 by 4 rows). In each box you'll write one word. Write it really small at the top so you leave yourself plenty of drawing room in the square. Write these words: weaving, active, broken, growing, echoing, spiraling, watery, random, climbing, bouncing, dancing, falling, running, wintry, furious, laughing. Inside each box you'll draw lines that represent each of these words.

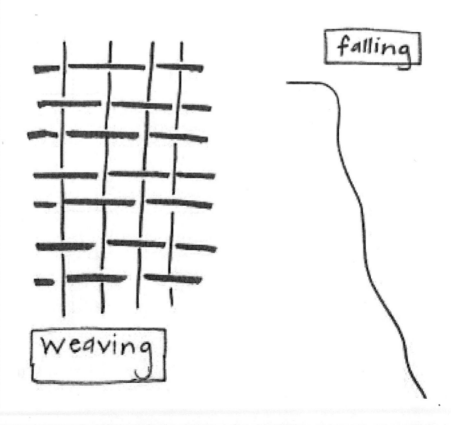

☺ ☻ ☻ **EXPLORATION: Feeling The Lines in Pictures**
Examine these two pictures. The first has strong vertical lines (the rows in the field) and the second has strong horizontal lines (the fence). Which is more restful and relaxing? Which feels more ordered and formal?

Create your own picture of a farmer's field. Try to achieve the opposite feeling from what is pictured above. Make the rows of your field run horizontally.

☺ ☻ ☻ **EXPLORATION: Leaving Lines**
The lines along this road in the painting on the next page are sometimes called "leaving lines." See how they narrow until they finally meet in a point as the road curves? That point where they meet is called the vanishing point. The lines coming together is what creates the illusion that the road is going off into the distance. Even simple lines are powerful in communicating ideas.

You can use lines to replicate the same technique. In your sketchbook, draw 2 lines traveling up your page, converging together until they meet at a single vanishing point. Practice making the road weaving in different directions, but always meeting in the vanishing point at the end.

Notice that the road fills almost the whole width of the page in the foreground. What is the effect when you make it fill either

---

Why So Emotional?

Most artists create in order to make a point. People respond much more readily to emotion than we do to a well reasoned essay . . . it's just the way we're wired. So everything about a painting from the colors to the composition to the medium are focused on eliciting your emotional responses.

Additional Layer

The Impressionist school of art rejected lines altogether. Check it out.

Fabulous Fact

The painting of the road in the Leaving Lines Exploration uses another trick to communicate distance that you may not have noticed. See how the colors change in the picture as your eye travels down the road? The trees in the foreground are darker, but get lighter in color further down the road. The actual color of the road does the same. This is partly to show the sunlight shining down, but it also helps tell us what parts of the picture are close and which are further away. Notice how light the colors are at the vanishing point.

Additional Layer

When you learn the history of the story behind a painting and what the various elements of a painting would have represented to the culture and time of the people who were contemporary with the artist, you gain a whole new understanding.

For example, *The Flower Carrier*, below and to the left, represents the oppression of the poor. The flowers were for the rich only, but the man "forced" to carry them is poor working class. In the painting he is literally oppressed and burdened by the rich.

Interestingly, Rivera was a communist.

Famous Folks

Diego Rivera was a Mexican artist who specialized in frescoes.

Photograph by Carl Van Vechten (1932)

more or less of the foreground on your sketches?

☺ ☻ EXPLORATION: Implied Lines

An implied line is not explicitly drawn, but it is suggested by points in the artwork. They are usually used to guide your eye to the main focus of the picture.

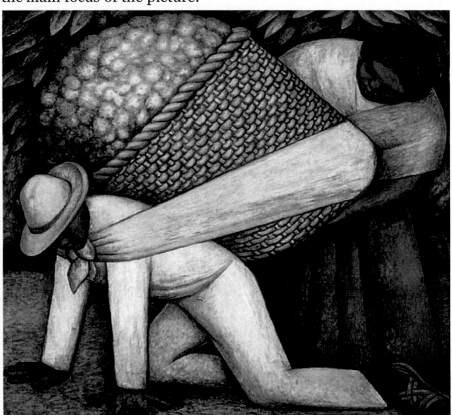

Diego Rivera's painting, *The Flower Carrier*, shows a very strong implied line. Can you see it? Look at the woman's gaze. Trace your finger from her eyes down to the man's face she is looking at. That is an implied line. The line is implied by the woman's gaze looking at the man. It makes us look down at the man too. The diagonal lines of the scarf holding the basket also direct our attention down toward the man's face along that same implied line.

Sometimes artists also draw a line that breaks off and then resumes; this becomes an implied line as well, and draws our eye to where the line leads. Look through an art book and see if you can spot any implied lines.

☺ ☻ EXPLORATION: Happily Ever After

Did you know that lines can tell a story? Drawing a story is very different than drawing a still life picture because in the story things are always changing. When you draw something or someone you can look at, it's a still life. When you are drawing a story it isn't still. It is dynamic, or active. You won't be drawing what your eyes see; you have to use your imagination.

For a great example of a line drawing story, read any of the Harold books by Crockett Johnson. A little boy named Harold goes on magnificent adventures using his purple crayon to tell his story. Read one of the Harold stories and point out how very simple lines are used. It doesn't look realistic, but it tells a great story.

Get a long roll of paper (or tape several sheets together or use freezer paper from the grocery store). Start on the left hand side of the page and draw along in a continuous way as Harold does. You can talk out loud and tell the story as you go. Before you begin, take a few minutes to decide on your topic and basic storyline so you won't get stuck in the middle. Here are a few ideas to get you started if you're stuck:

- My Best Day Ever
- When I'm Grown Up
- Last Night I Dreamed
- On My Summer Vacation
- On My Birthday
- If I Were in Charge of the World
- My Day At The Zoo

You can write a title along the top of your page or vertically on the

---

Additional Layer

Leaving lines and vanishing points aren't just for dirt roads. Try using the same principles to draw rivers, railroad tracks, a busy cityscape, and anything else that travels off into the distance.

There are several vanishing points in this painting by George Inness. Can you find them?

Additional Layer

Stories have a beginning, middle, and end. Identify those parts in your line stories.

Additional Layer

Learn about pseudonyms. Crockett Johnson's real name was David Johnson Leisk. Crockett was a childhood nickname that stuck. Leisk was too hard to pronounce so he stuck with Johnson. Let all the kids come up with their own cool pseudonym.

Discuss some reasons that authors use pseudonyms instead of their own given names.

On the Web
Two cool sites to help you learn more about great art and artists:

http://www.color-me-online.com/masterpiece/index.html

http://www.classicsforkids.com/

Expedition

Got an art museum or gallery near you? Take a field trip after you've learned about lines and look for the use of lines in the art you see.

Additional Layer
Look at some children's books by Marcia Brown. She utilizes a printmaking technique similar to the textured prints exploration for much of her stellar artwork. You can see the repetition of lines that create texture throughout her illustrations.

On the Web
Watch this art school video on line:http://youtu.be/po3EFoQ9MyU
Use real art supplies like a real art class . . . cool.

left hand edge. The story can be told either by spreading the whole paper out, or by being rolled up in a scroll, and then unrolled as the story is told.

☺ ☻ ☻ EXPLORATION: Moving Lines
Look at some comic strips and spot small lines that cartoonists use to show movement or action. These tiny action lines bring the simple line characters to life. Cartoonists use very simple lines to make their pictures come alive.

Brainstorm a list of verbs and write them down. Make sure you include both active and passive verbs. Active verbs have a lot of movement and energy (like run, jump, dance, fall, etc.). Passive verbs have lower intensities (like dream, rest, think, watch). Next to each of your verbs, draw a small action line that represents the verb.

Tell someone about the actions you chose and the lines you drew to represent those actions. Which are high-energy and which are low-energy? Do your lines reflect that? Compare your lines with someone else's – are they the same?

☺ ☻ ☻ EXPLORATION: Emoticons
Emoticons and graphical emoticons on the computer are commonly used to send an implied tone along with a message.

For example, I may YELL AT YOU ONLINE!! But if I follow it up with a wink ;) then my yelling becomes a joke.

Each of these graphical emoticons is so similar, but they use slight changes in tiny lines to send clear messages. What is the difference between the first face and the second? The exact same lines are used, but they convey two different emotions. What did the artist do to change *happy* to *sad*? Now look at the third face. What emotion does it represent? What lines did the artist use to create that emotion?

Draw a series of your own emoticons. Pay attention to what tiny lines do to communicate different emotions. See if someone can guess which emotions you drew.

☺ ☺ ☻ EXPLORATIONS: Textured Prints

When lines or shapes are repeated over and over again, they can create textures. To see this in action, get a clean Styrofoam meat tray and a pencil. If the edges of your tray are raised you should cut off the raised edges so it's easier to work with.

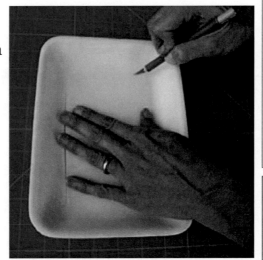

First, come up with a simple to draw item that has texture: a basketball, a fish, a flower, a pumpkin — whatever you'd like. Sketch the item in your sketchbook, and remember to add in repeating lines to create the texture. A basketball would have repeating dots; a fish would have small repeating curves to show the scales; you get the idea. Once you like the way it looks, lightly sketch it on the Styrofoam tray. Now deepen your sketch lines to create nice, deep grooves everywhere you want the lines and textures to show. This is your printmaking template.

Choose a color of construction paper and a contrasting paint color. Paint the flat surface of Styrofoam (without painting inside the grooves) and then quickly stamp it down on to the construction paper, creating your textured print. Simple lines create texcture.

☺ ☺ ☻ EXPLORATION: Shape Builders

Take turns drawing a shape on a piece of paper or a white board. Come up with as many shapes as you can until you've run out of ideas. You likely started by drawing geometric shapes. Now add to your list. Add some everyday shapes, like the outline of a

On The Web

To watch the process of how different kinds of prints are made go to http://www/mom.org/wxhibitions/2001/whatisaprint/flash.html

Additional Layer

Look up at the sky on a cloudy day. What shapes do you see in the clouds? Are you more likely to spot geometric or organic shapes when you're cloud gazing?

Explanation

When I teach the arts I have a few goals in mind:

1. Expose kids to great art and music, learning about the artists and musicians along the way.

2. Teach them the principles real artists use (line, shape, unity, balance, color, etc.)

3. Let them have real experiences and practice

4. Allow them to be creative and unhindered by too many rules

This is accomplished by learning about a particular piece of art, discussing the elements and style of the piece, then learning about the artist's life, and finally by trying out the artist's techniques on our own.

Sometimes we do just-for-fun projects like making lip gloss or bead sculptures. I also let my kids do a lot of art projects just for fun all on their own. They have a scrap box filled with artsy types of things-- paper, stickers, old tins, bottles, boxes, fabric, yarn, pipe cleaners, shoe boxes, wiggly eyes, bottle caps, and anything else I find to throw in there.

Karen

house, a leaf, a person, a spoon, or a table. What do your shape drawings have in common?

A shape is the outline of a form that is COMPLETELY closed. It has to be able to be drawn with one continuous line. Can you spot the one that is NOT a shape?

Are there other shapes you could add to your list? Is it possible to ever run out of options?

Here's a little quiz. See if you can get 100%.

1. How do lines make shapes?
   (They go all the way around the outside of a form.)
2. What part of a form is the shape?
   (The outside, or the edges)
3. Point at the shapes you drew that are geometric. Now point at the shapes that represent something (everyday shapes). Now point at the nonsense shapes.

☺ ☻ EXPLORATION: Sponge Shapes

Often we look at something we want to draw or paint and think it would be way too hard for us. If you look closely though, you'll see that many things are made up of simple shapes. Cut a sponge into some simple shapes of various sizes. Dip the sponge into paint and print the shape on a sheet of paper. Here's a hint – start with the biggest shape first so you'll be able to layer the smaller shapes on top to create detail.

Here are a few things you could create:
- a house, barn, schoolhouse, or church
- a graveyard

- a tree (or even a Christmas tree)
- a flower
- a fish, bear, dog, cat, or bunny rabbit
- a person
- a boat, train, car, or plane

What shapes did you use?

☺ ☺ ☺ EXPLORATION: Terrific Tangrams

Print out a tangram from the printables at the end of this unit. Carefully cut apart the shape pieces and use the shapes to create pictures. Here are a few examples:

Can you make a sailboat? A tree? A fish? A house? A person? A duck? What else can you make? Here are a few more to try:

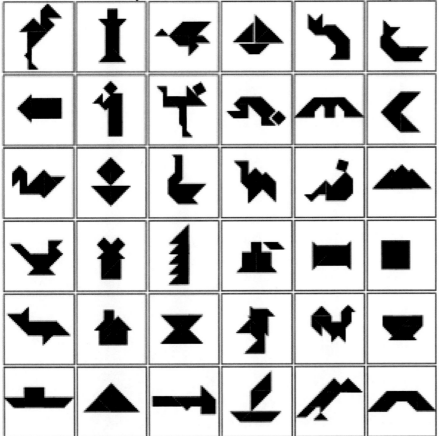

The traditional tangram rules say:
1. All 7 pieces must be used.
2. All pieces must lie flat.
3. All pieces must touch.
4. No pieces may overlap.
5. Pieces may be rotated or flipped as needed.
You can use these rules, or be more flexible! Traditionally, only

Famous Folks

Raphael Sanzio was a Florentine painter of the Renaissance. He died at only 37 years old, but left a huge body of work behind nevertheless.

Self-portrait (1506)

Famous Folks

Pablo Picasso was a Spanish painter and founder of the innovative cubist movement in art. Cubism uses mostly geometric shapes to create interesting art.

1962, from Wikimedia Commons

Additional Layer

Gather a variety of art supplies like pipe cleaners, yarn, popsicle sticks, rubber bands, straws, and twist ties. Glue the objects on to construction paper to create pictures. Create a scene like an underwater scene, a farm, or your house only using the objects as your lines.

Additional Layer

Pablo Picasso wasn't so natural when he used shapes. Find some of his art on the internet or in an art book. His style, called cubism, used shapes much more literally.

Additional Layer

Triangles were the most commonly used shape during the Renaissance. Triangles are strong, attractive, and balanced. They also utilize the number 3, which represents importance. Christians especially used triangles, as they referenced the trinity. The number 3 has always held a lot of sway in religious, artistic, and scientific communities. There are most definitely elements of science and symbolism in good art.

one tangram set can be used at a time, but if you want to create more elaborate pictures you can print more.

Using tangrams, we utilized geometric shapes to create organic forms. We can often spot geometric shapes even within organic ones. Beginning how-to-draw books and websites often have budding artists begin by drawing geometric shapes and then smoothing them together to create more lifelike pictures.

☺ ☻ ☻ EXPLORATION: Moving Rubbings

When artists repeat shapes they can make it seem as though they are moving across the page. You can make the shape walk, jump, run, wander, or even fly across the page.

Choose a shape and draw it on a thick piece of card stock or a manilla folder. It can be a circle, square, triangle, bee, butterfly, fish, or other animal – any shape that you want to have move. Cut out the shape carefully, trying to keep the edges nice and smooth.

Now get a blank sheet of paper or your sketchbook. Place your shape stencil underneath the paper, beginning on one edge. Rub over it with a crayon so your shape appears. Now move it a little bit and do another rubbing. Keep doing this until your shape has moved across the page. Keep in mind what kind of movement pattern you should create. A bunny rabbit will not move the same way a snake would.

☻ ☻ EXPLORATION: Literal or Natural

Famous artists throughout time have used shape. Sometimes it's very natural and can be hard to spot. Other times it's quite literal.

Raphael's Madonna has natural shapes. The shape of the arrangement of their bodies is triangular. Baby Jesus has a very rectangular shape. You can see the triangle and the rectangle if you look closely. The geometric shapes overlaying the picture on the following page show you how you can spot geometry even in natural shapes:

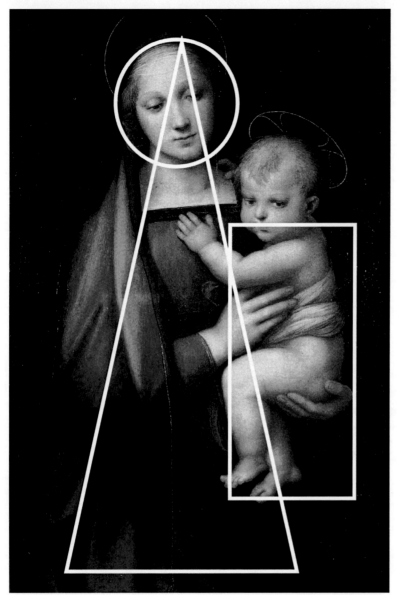

Look through an art book and see what shapes, both natural and literal, you can find.

Teaching Tip

We can't say enough how much we love "How-to-Draw" books for teaching kids. Kids begin to see the shapes in everyday objects and realize a great depiction is just a series of the right lines. These simple books also give kids confidence in their art abilities.

Begin every art lesson with a quick how-to-draw tutorial and watch as their drawing ability and confidence shoots up.

You can find inexpensive basic drawing books online, check some out from the library, or just do a google search for "How to draw _____"

(fill in whatever thing is wildly interesting to your kids at the moment). You may want to pull from other studies. For example, while learning about mountains, learn to draw them as well.

Coming up next . . .

Unit 1-12

Arabia
Rivers & Lakes
Atoms - Color & Value

My Ideas For This Unit:

Title: _____   Topic: _____

_____

_____

_____

_____

_____

_____

_____

_____

_____

Title: _____   Topic: _____

_____

_____

_____

_____

_____

_____

_____

_____

_____

_____

Title: _____   Topic: _____

_____

_____

_____

_____

_____

_____

_____

_____

My Ideas For This Unit:

Title: _____   Topic: _____

_____

_____

_____

_____

_____

_____

_____

_____

_____

Title: _____   Topic: _____

_____

_____

_____

_____

_____

_____

_____

_____

_____

Title: _____   Topic: _____

_____

_____

_____

_____

_____

_____

_____

_____

Japanese Temple

This is a gateway to a Japanese temple complex. This one is Buddhist, but the Shinto shrines look much the same. This temple is not for people to worship in, it is to store artifacts and to be a place for the monks to live and work. The Japanese do not worship in special buildings like westerners. Japanese architecture is made of wood, raised slightly from the ground, and has tile roofs. The gently curved roof dominates the building and is typical of Japanese architecture.

Early Japan: Unit I-II

14000-300BC |-||

Jomon Period

660 BC |-||

The Mythical Emperor Jimmu, a descendant of the Sun Goddess, founds the royal dynasty

300BC-250AD |-||

Yayoi Period; weaving, rice farming, and working in iron and bronze begin

57 AD |-||

Japan first mentioned in Chinese records

220 AD |-||

Queen Himiko is chosen to bring peace to the warring Wa (Japanese) tribes, uniting them for the first time

250AD-538AD |-||

Kofun Period; strong military states emerge

538 AD |-||

Buddhism is introduced to Japan by this date

538 - 710 AD |-||

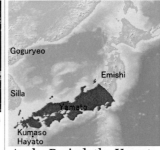

Goguryeo

Emishi

Silla

Yamato

Kumaso
Hayato

Asuka Period; the Yamato unite and rule most of Japan

594 AD |-||

Prince Shotoku rules for Empress Suiko and works to spread Chinese religion and culture

710 AD |-||

The capital is moved from Asuka to Nara and the Nara period begins; the empire becomes centralized; the emperor becomes a figurehead

Ancient Japan c. 600 AD

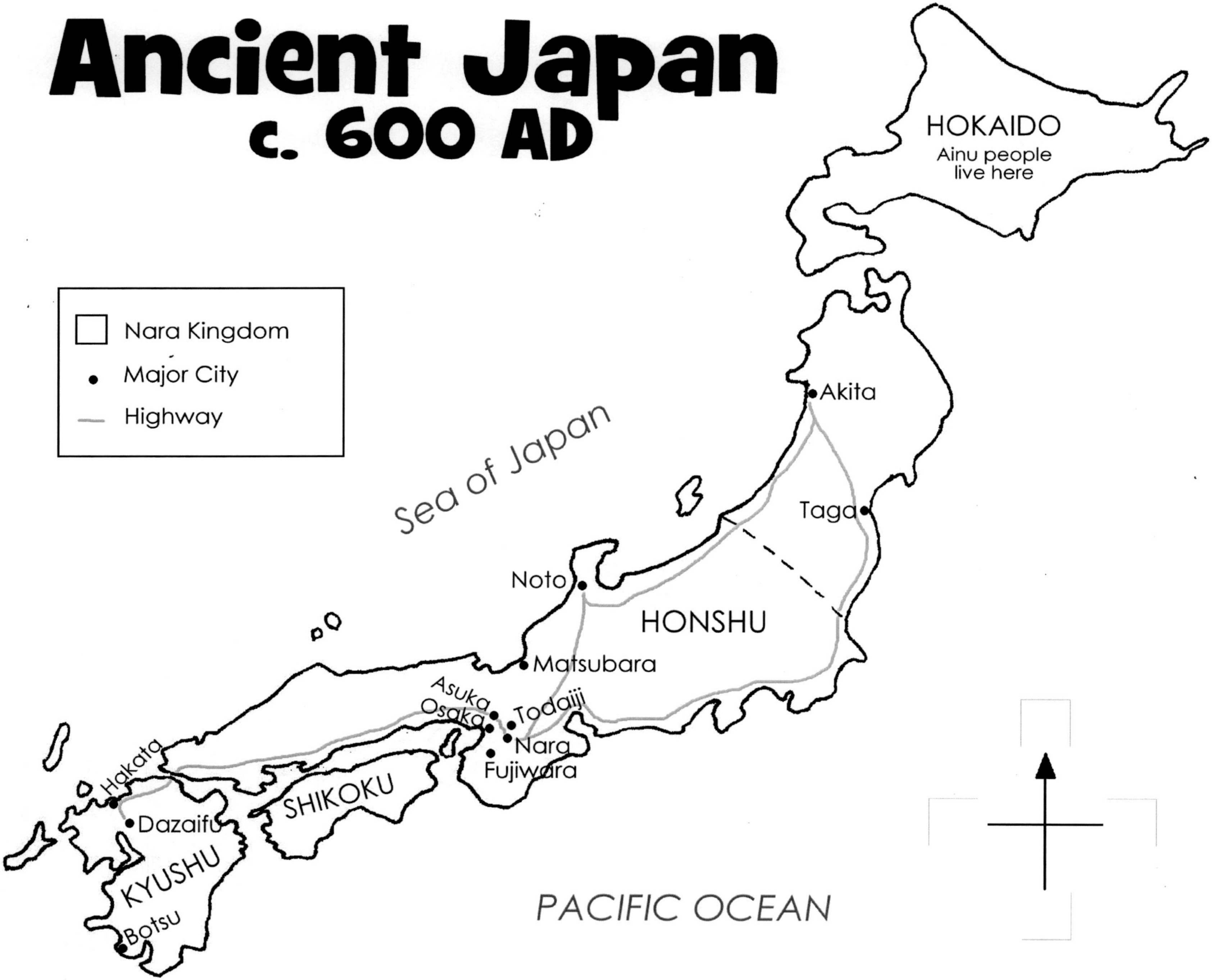

HOKAIDO
Ainu people
live here

HONSHU

Akita

Taga

Noto

Matsubara

Todaiji

Asuka
Osaka
Nara
Fujiwara

SHIKOKU

KYUSHU

Dazaifu

Hakata

Botsu

Sea of Japan

PACIFIC OCEAN

Nara Kingdom

• Major City

— Highway

The World

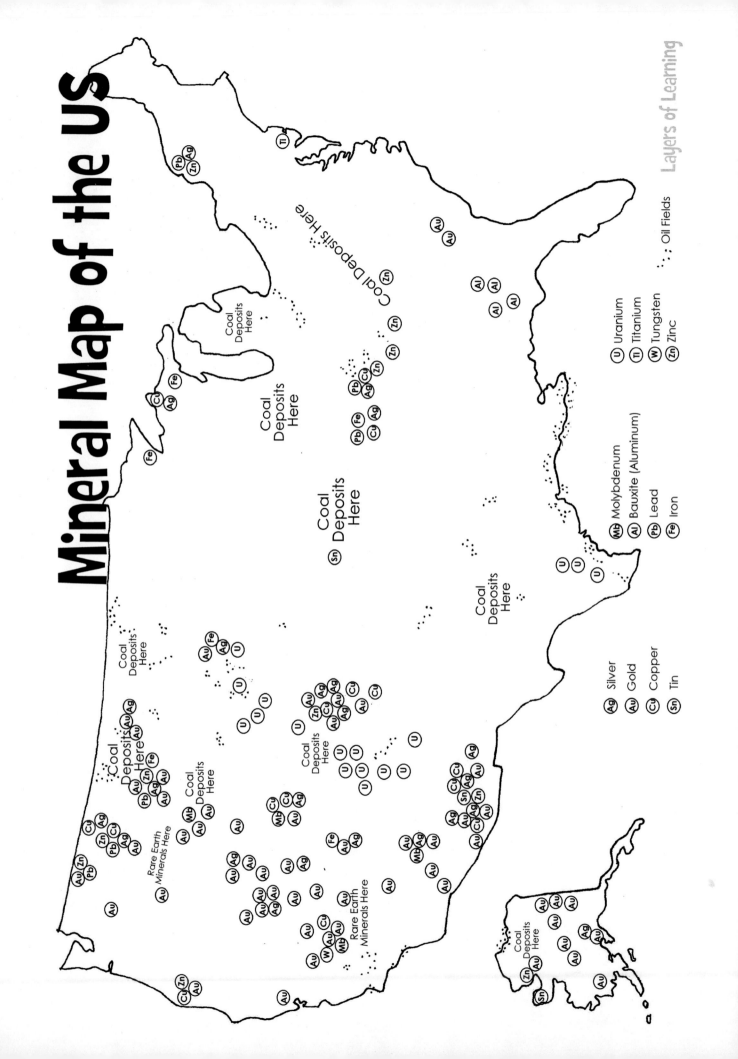

Mineral Map of the US

Layers of Learning

Coal Deposits Here

Coal Deposits Here

Coal Deposits Here

Coal Deposits Here

Coal Deposits Here

Coal Deposits Here

Coal Deposits Here

Coal Deposits Here

Coal Deposits Here

Rare Earth Minerals Here

Rare Earth Minerals Here

·.· Oil Fields

(U) Uranium
(Ti) Titanium
(W) Tungsten
(Zn) Zinc

(Mo) Molybdenum
(Al) Bauxite (Aluminum)
(Pb) Lead
(Fe) Iron

(Ag) Silver
(Au) Gold
(Cu) Copper
(Sn) Tin

Cougar, mountain lion, or panther: lives in a wide range from jungle to high mountains in the Americas. Eats anything it can catch.

Mountain goat: lives in the northern Rockies and Cascade Range of North America. Can be very aggressive and dangerous.

Ptarmigan: lives on high elevations, eating berries, buds, leaves, seeds and flowers. Does not migrate, turning snowy white in the winter.

Pika: live on rocky mountain slopes. They cut hay from grasses, lay it out to dry, and then store it in underground burrows for the winter.

Ermine: also known as a stoat, this animal is brown in the summer and pure white with a black tipped tail in the winter.

Tangram

Use the tangram to create cool shape pictures. Traditionally only one set is used at a time, but if you want to create more elaborate pictures you can print several. Print them on to colored cardstock and laminate them to use over and over again.

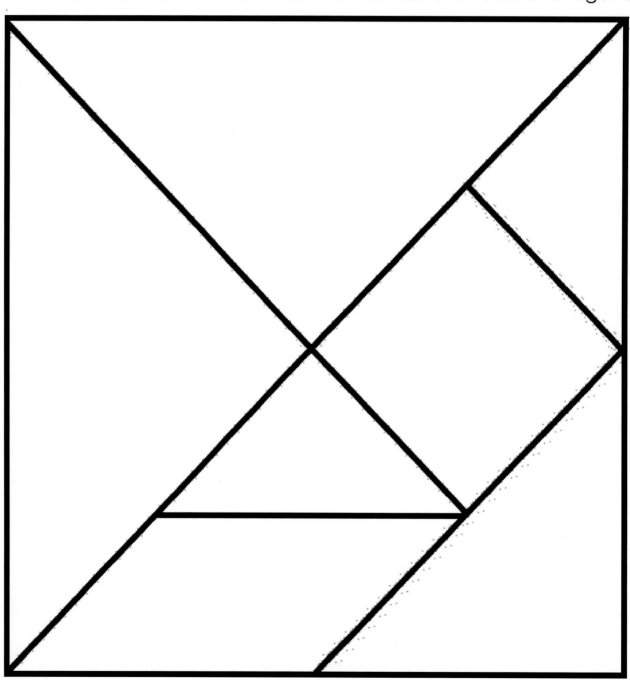

ABOUT THE AUTHORS

Karen & Michelle . . .
Mothers, sisters, teachers, women who are passionate
about educating kids.
We are dedicated to lifelong learning.

Karen, a mother of four, who has homeschooled her kids for more than eight years with her husband, Bob, has a bachelor's degree in child development with an emphasis in education. She lives in Utah where she gardens, teaches piano, and plays an excruciating number of board games with her kids. Karen is our resident Arts expert and English guru {most necessary as Michelle regularly and carelessly mangles the English language and occasionally steps over the bounds of polite society}.

Michelle and her husband, Cameron, homeschooling now for over a decade, teach their six boys on their ten acres in beautiful Idaho country. Michelle earned a bachelor's in biology, making her the resident Science expert, though she is mocked by her friends for being the *Botanist with the Black Thumb of Death*. She also is the go-to for History and Government. She believes in staying up late, hot chocolate, and a no whining policy. We both pitch in on Geography, in case you were wondering, and are on a continual quest for knowledge.

*Visit our constantly updated blog for tons of free ideas,
free printables, and more cool stuff for sale:*
www.Layers-of-Learning.com